AFTER HOURS

FOR SAXOPHONE AND PIANO

GW00771213

PAM WEDGWOOD

FABER *ff* MUSIC

CONTENTS

The accompaniment CD: Each piece in this *After Hours* collection has two different backing tracks: the first ('full performance') includes the backing track along with the instrumental melody; the second ('backing only') presents the backing track alone. The 'full performance' track is provided to help the player to learn the melody and its interaction with the accompaniment; the melody is played on a vibraphone to avoid dominating the acoustic 'live' instrument for those players who choose to play along with this version of the backing.

© 2004 by Faber Music Ltd
First published in 2004 by Faber Music Ltd
Bloomsbury House 74–77 Great Russell Street London WC1B 3DA
Music processed by MusicSet 2000
Cover by Velladesign
Printed in England by Caligraving Ltd
All rights reserved

ISBN10: 0-571-52266-1
EAN13: 978-0-571-52266-8

CD recorded at House of Music Studio
Produced by Kathryn Oswald and Sam Wedgwood
Engineered by Sam Wedgwood
℗ 2004 by Faber Music Ltd
© 2004 by Faber Music Ltd

To buy Faber Music publications or to find out about the full range of titles available
please contact your local music retailer or Faber Music sales enquiries:

Faber Music Limited, Burnt Mill, Elizabeth Way, Harlow, CM20 2HX England
Tel: +44 (0)1279 82 89 82   Fax: +44 (0)1279 82 89 83
sales@fabermusic.com   fabermusic.com

CALL IT A DAY

Pam Wedgwood

3 full performance
4 backing only

SLIDING DOORS

Pam Wedgwood

With a strong rhythmic feel ♩ = 132 – 144

THE FRIENDS

Pam Wedgwood

REMEMBER WHEN

Pam Wedgwood

9 full performance
10 backing only

SUMMER NIGHTS

Pam Wedgwood

full performance
backing only

COME DANCE WITH ME

Pam Wedgwood

FALLING

Pam Wedgwood

13 full performance
14 backing only

SURVIVOR

Pam Wedgwood